Girl Reading a Letter at an Open Window

Jeffrey Bean

Girl Reading a Letter at an Open Window
Winner of the 2013 Cowles/Copperdome Poetry Chapbook
Competition

First publication 2014 by
Southeast Missouri State University Press
One University Plaza, MS 2650
Cape Girardeau, MO 63701

Cover Photo by Bradley Phillips
Cover Design by Carrie M. Walker
Page Design by Lilly Bange

ISBN: 978-0-9883103-91

For Jessica

And for Olivia

Contents

Acknowledgments

Grateful acknowledgement is made to the editors of the following publications in which the poems listed below first appeared:

Ascent:	At the Chippewa Nature Reserve
Bateau:	The one you learned to hope for
Cider Press Review:	Letters
Cimarron Review:	I don't live in the kind of house
Crab Orchard Review:	Alfred Sisley: *Snow at Louveciennes*
Drunken Boat:	Portrait of Two Friends Wrestling
The Fiddleback:	Summer Garden
Juked:	The Joy of Painting
	Newborn
Memorious:	Your Hands on This Rail
Redivider:	Parable of the Lice
RHINO:	Love brought me down again
Smartish Pace:	It's Morning in Michigan
Southern Poetry Review:	Weeds
Subtropics:	The Bread
	Why I Quit Playing Text-Twist
Swink:	On TV
	What Geraniums Smell Like

Many thanks go to Central Michigan University for their support of this project, and especially to my creative writing colleagues, Robert Fanning, Darrin Doyle, and Matt Roberson—amazing teachers, writers, and friends. Thanks to my fantastic editor, Susan Swartwout, for her attention to this project, and for dreaming up the cover; thanks to Bradley Phillips for the brilliant cover photo; and thanks to everyone at Southeast Missouri State University Press. Finally, sincere thanks go to my family, especially Barbara and John Bean, David Bean and Jini Puma, Carole and Eddie Powell, and the rest of the Powell clan, for their love and support; and to Jessica and Olivia, for everything.

The Bread

The bread, the salad, simple, oiled.
  The coats on hooks, exhaling winter smoke.
The hand that was mine, the knuckles, the table, smooth oak.
  The girl I'd come to meet, the sky behind her hair, *shook foil*.

Her legs crossed at the ankles, the coiling
  evening traffic, forgettable talk.
The oysters, fat men at the bar, laughs like question marks
  of breath. The salt on the roads she came down, the choice

she made, the choice she almost made,
  her mouth there, where I could touch it.
 What we tasted, smelled, said,
the places on my body she touched, the places she did not.
  I had been lonely, I had been hungry as a rat.
The glass, the salt, the road, her hands, the bread.

Your Hands on This Rail

Your hands on this rail
poised like a pianist's

are birds in the slow movies
my father shot with his super 8,

jays that live now only on film,
hanging forever in the breezes of the 80s,

the dust of those summers
that stuck in my mouth

like the retainer I'd pluck out
to point at girls on the playground,

a disembodied organ, pink as sex, alive
as the moths I cupped in my hands,

the pulses and smudges they left with me,
their ashy vanishings into that pasture

in Iowa, full of cricket fire,
that held my house and the day

in my twenties you lay on my bed,
peeled off your socks, lifted your throat

up to me, the image of your skin
folding in and in me where

it is still coiled, like a reel of film,
waiting to be threaded through light.

Why I Quit Playing Text-Twist

I kept missing *her*. Like in *whiner*,
where I also missed *wren* and *whir*.
I couldn't find *womb* in *bowman*. In *gusted*
I uncovered *dust* and *sued*, but not *duets*.
Who wouldn't find *bile*, *bite*, and *lie*
in *blithe*? It's harder to find
lite and *lithe*. In *snares*
I missed *seas*. Every kid has found *girls*
in *grills* by accident, but not me. I only
got *lugs* and *ugly* in *snugly*, made up *gunsly*.
I saw *sewers* but not *seers*, the *hole*
in *behold*. There *she* was in *pusher*,
lurking with the *user*, but I missed *her*
again, and the *pure* there, the *hue*.

Love brought me down again

to these train tracks, the ties swollen
with summer heat, the ballast rocks glittering
with shattered things, even in the dark.
The graffiti I carved into the grass
has vanished, but the grass insists
on whispering about it. Soon
the train will grind past, hauling
its flammables into the heart
of the city, fences, red lights,
signs that say danger,
cages inside cages where
the coal goes in, the hot feelers
of wires stretch out to the house
where she sleeps, fill it with buzzes
and glow. I will walk the tracks
until I pass her backyard, suck
her lights out through her window.
I will fall asleep with a piece of coal
in my fist like a syllable until morning
when she comes out for the mail
and I open my hand, holding up that
one word, silent and brought here to burn.

Vermeer: *Couple Standing at a Virginal*

The girl's fingers slide along
the virginal's keys,
pull triads into air.
The man kneads
his cane against his palm.
Her face in the mirror opens—
toward him? Away?
He wishes she were bread
he could hold on his tongue.
The artist has left a place
for you, an empty chair.
The viola de gamba
lies silent on the floor,
wears silence like
a skirt you could unwrap
if you would kneel down
between the couple,
take the soft wood in
your arms. Can you feel
the notes you don't play?
They slide like fingers
along the skin
of the room.

Remember the Storm

I study the weather map, looking for you
as though green swaths of rain on the radar
were your hair and smell about to wash
over my city, like you could be predicted,
graphed, and I could dress right, or leave town,
before you blew against my coast, breaking
record highs, the white foam of you
pounding me, my sandy body drinking
your salt, like I could stand outside,
open my mouth, catch you on my tongue,
and you'd become my tendons and pigments, cells
and lipids, the grease I leave on pillows,
earpieces of phones, and forever they would say,
remember the storm, and every year every kid
in school would learn to sing your name.

What Geraniums Smell Like

Like birds.
Like my brother leaving for the lake.
Like the smudge of fireworks on driveways.
Like breath trapped in a canteen.
Like the word *breath*.
Like mice.
Like want.
Like a nickel in a fist.
Like my brother leaving for the store.
Like my brother leaving for the war.
Like a handful of washed hair.
Like my mom humming Johnny Cash.
Like a red towel in the wash.
Like a scrape on a thigh.
Like a Service Merchandise.
Like my dad's violin.
Like a cloth that cleans guns.
Like car leather.
Like a war turned low on a radio.
Like parents getting used to you gone.
Like baby I love you.
Like you are the only one.
Like holes in the knees of jeans.
Like what you weren't supposed to see.
Like drops of blood on a hardwood floor.
Like my brother leaving for the war.
Like ice in a glass.
Like beets.
Like leaving.
Like, *please*.
Like bees.

Weeds

Black amber, purple loosestrife,
  shattercane—when I was ten, whatever curled
    and broke the yards was in my book a good curse.

By train tracks, behind barns,
  splitting sidewalks beside strip malls,
    they bloomed. I waded and touched what I could:

The hairy stems of burcucumber,
  Columbus grass, the white flash of hoary alyssum.
    Where responsible men had not yet put poison

I moved, I floated like milkweed.
  And I loved those weeds, their recklessness,
    their hunger, the urges that split them open.

Like them, I did everything careless:
  I slouched, I drank the air, I haunted
    edges and alleys, leaning for the sunshine, dumb.

Portrait of Two Friends Wrestling

We wrestle on couches, wrestle on carpets,
wrestle in cars, crash flesh into flesh,
wrestle in chairs, wrestle to music,
make up new moves, we wrestle and cry,
wrestle ourselves, wrestle in sleep,
wrestle like counterpoint
sung in a church,
wrestle to eat, wrestle to praise,
wrestle to talk, to pray, to drink, we wrestle
for money, wrestle with books,
wrestle in mall fountains, banks,
we scuff up the clean floors of hospitals,
wrestle with breath, wrestle like trains
across states, away from the chest,
away from the arms, away from the hair, the hands,
until who we were wrestling is only a thought
we wrestle in air, as close as we can.

Parable of the Lice

Everybody knows the lice are lonely.
And yet we go baring
our hairy necks in the park,
screaming down hills
on bicycles. The image
of the down on our legs
burns all night in their heads.
What tiny fire, that thought!
It is fire the color of our blood,
it is made of it, it is the color
of our bodies drenched
in early sunlight.
It is thinking like this
that makes them lonely.

On TV

On TV a model flashed
her hands out under the lights,
made her body slippery
as a ruby. What the hell

had I done worth two shits
was what I thought my beer
can would say to me with its
nasally little song if it sang.

Answer: I had watched turkey
buzzards make their arcs
above untold quantities of corn.
My body was an armchair.

My body might roll out toward the banks
of the loud night like a wave, it might
dance like cellophane in traffic, it might flash
green as TVs against windows.

My beer can closed its eye
and sang upside down a new
TV-name for me, a lovely
sound, out under the lights, far.

Vermeer: *Girl Reading a Letter at an Open Window*

She wills her body to hold still
against the tug and shove of cloth.
The bunched-up tapestry on the table
spills a bowl of fruit turning soft,

shrinking in shadows cast by her dress.
The paper in her hands looks ruined,
her face is mute. The lion heads
carved on the chair, the sash, the curtains—

all push close to read the news.
We know it's bad. The window knows
how light and all of us get used:
her curls, reflected, look like bones.

No floor, no ceiling in this room.
She's young. She's almost gone.

Summer Garden

It failed: I kept spading the dirt into
the shape of her hair. Nothing grew. That winter
each day I did a spell: I wrote down what she said,
folded the notes into my pocket, went skiing
in the forest so her breath when she came home
smelled like a katabatic wind
blasting pines. We kissed one night
on the couch, the TV preacher
broke down, finally, said something
so powerful and strange
we wouldn't have needed to fall in love,
but we didn't hear it, not fully, and she went on
buying me beautiful shirts, my closet like
a hothouse, flowers so red I can't sleep.

The one you learned to hope for

is out buying sandwiches.
You scrub tomato sauce off a bright pot.
She has written a poem thanking the chair and floor
for buoying her up, keeping her body from crashing
down into the cellar, and she is going to read it.
A man comes pounding on your door at 3 am,
scared in the wind, pretending to need
the phone. Nothing comes of it. She and you go on
eating popcorn, moving from lit rooms
to dark rooms. No matter how dark it gets
you can still feel shapes, and sometimes
in her sleep she cries out like a hinge. All winter
you watch the neighbor shovel his walk, jealous
of his coat. Nights when she falls asleep before you,
you thank the floor, then her body, then your body
for keeping you buoyed and warm and apart.

Letters

They arrive through the mail slot, smelling of thumbs,
with the charged freshness of produce, or wings
just cut from a living thing.

They are blind in their bushels,
they do not know what makes their bodies light.
They hurtle over oceans and ice.

They move over roads so long
they turn like roads into names.
They cannot see their names,

they do not understand their clothes,
only that they close to the one face they know
then open to a strange face. Then close.

They come warm to tables
like peppered bread, white, black.
Like us, they do not understand

how they nourish—only that
something swallows them like savory food.
They dream of the time they were meaningless wood.

Newborn

My baby is a chubby fire, flaring
all night into the eye of
the video monitor. Birds love her,
call back when she cries them awake
at five a.m. A father
now, I understand birds,
how unbearably thin
their voices are. I will write
in the book of her life
that I swung her up, thumped
with love her plump back,
cleaned and kissed her feet,
played the heavy banjo
of her sobs, stormed through
the upstairs rooms with box fans
all June to cool her down.
I'll never tell her I cried into my eggs
for my old life, or the dream
where she's my thumb grown enormous,
heavy at the end of my arm,
and I have to shred with my one good hand
my endless hair to feed her.

At the Chippewa Nature Reserve

By the front desk at the visitor center
encased in glass there is a river otter,
stuffed, that my one-year-old daughter
knows how to talk to. She kneels there,
hands pressed to the glass, and the otter
listens to her handful of syllables. I want her
to be asking the otter, "who brought your
face back to life, how do you look forever
up at lights like that?" But she can't say "er"
or any sound with "r," and she doesn't wonder
what I like to think she wonders. The otter
and she understand each other,
they both look up as I say their names, their
mouths opening, right on the verge of words.

I don't live in the kind of house

that in a pizza commercial would sell you pizzas.
For one thing you wouldn't like the colors of the walls,
and by you I mean you pizza lovers, dialing the numbers
on your phone right now, readying your tongue
to recite your list of toppings, and the problem with the colors
is that they're too dark for you, deep reds and deep blues,
and the wall sockets are plugged up with child-proof thingies
so my daughter doesn't stab in her finger and blow herself up,
my daughter who is incredibly sharp, she learned to clap
just by watching my wife clap, she brought her fingers together
and found a kind of safe electricity there that made her hungry.
She would have ordered a pizza if she could speak English,
she can almost say pizza but that doesn't cut it with Dominos,
what cuts it with them is money, crisp and folded, and you there
are now moving your money toward the hot cheese that zooms
at your doorbell in a car with brakes so bad even my daughter,
whose name is Olivia, who claps the way Chuck Berry plays guitar,
even she hears the sorrow in that metal scraping up to your door
past the brand new houses whose windows alone could sell you
a fucking triple-decker double-cheese goat meat pie with avocado.

The Joy of Painting

Before bed, I'm watching Bob Ross
(you know, the painter guy on PBS)
and I notice the sun spots on his hand
as he swirls with the fan brush. And those spots
make me think how he is going to die someday
(actually, I realize, he *is* dead by now) and that
makes me think an old, tired thought: how my baby
upstairs asleep will grow up to die, and by then
if things go as planned I'll be dead and my wife
too, but tonight on TV Bob Ross is happy
and alive, using odorless paint thinner, saying
let your imagination run wild and *let it go,*
here, you can do anything that you want to,
and he's making a huge mountain struck by light,
and in the face of this and the death all over
his hands, I'm drinking warm milk and hoping
I can drift off to sleep without trouble. And Bob
is washing his brush now, and drying it, saying,
just beat the devil out of it, and now he's painting
a happy little tree, almost like the one he imagined.

Vermeer: *Woman Putting on Pearls*

Sometimes you get a minute or two,
nobody needs you for once, your body's buoyed
by that grass-and-river feeling after lunch,
you draw back the shutters and the room
takes on the freshness of streams, hard buds
swelling up outside. It's early spring,
you've got your best coat on, ermine trim,
and you lift up a necklace to the light,
to the space and quiet (it's a gift, it asks
to be touched like this), and the places it touches
you, fingertips and throat, become
organs more sensitive than mirrors or eyes.
The V the ribbon makes that holds the pearls
draws the pleasures of the room in closer:
this chair, this table, this blue rug, the tug
of your earrings, your hair bow like a pink, chubby hand,
the downward slope of your forearms, eyelids,
mouth, light all over the wall like words
for what you wanted, words you can't remember
now that you're thinking what the light is *really*,
shattering fire, violent as birth
for billions of years out there in space, that long,
blue-cold cloth, an emptiness from which
sometimes come moons pink as hands in orbit
around a throat, a head, some pearls, warm for now.

Curls of Smoke

They look soft,
you said, those curls of smoke
above Philadelphia

we saw out the window
of our plane, leaving
the fires of that city,

the wedding of our good friends,
all of that glad crying and yelling,
that tightness in our chests.

What made the smoke,
I asked you, jet trails, ship exhaust,
some kind of suburb fire,

leaf piles going up, or was it
layers, smoke on top of smoke
from several places?

Then we flew into the smoke,
and you saw, you said,
fields and trees

down through it, their colors
changed by it, and it made
you think of the groomsmen,

somehow, our childhood friends
getting fat, sneaking drinks
while their wives were away,

and the ridiculous fight
the bride and groom had
on the wedding night,

the songs we had wept to
still inside them,
the embarrassing speeches

and dance moves
of their fathers:
they were arguing over condoms,

who had lost them,
they told us the next day,
and laughed at it then,

but the night of the fight each wanted the other
to feel how hard it had been,
enduring the shame and hope

of the ceremony, the lilies, the shoulders
of bridesmaids, the noise of rain
on the outdoor pavilion

so loud the homily got lost in it
and the reverend asked God
if it pleased Him, please hold it back,

the rain, but it didn't please Him,
we guessed, because the roar grew,
and we all laughed or strained

to catch what he was saying,
the words of blessing for these two,
wanting to hear

how we too might be blessed,
how we might be courageous
enough to raise our kids,

to love or strain enough to make it
together to death.
When I'm dead, you said,

looking down now at the curls of smoke,
throw me from an airplane, into the fields
and trees. My ashes, I mean.

It's Morning in Michigan

                      and I want to praise the bottoms
of the boots of college girls, I want to ride out
on the breath they pass into the mouths of boys
they love.
                 In last night's dream I was coffee, all of my heat
rolled upward into steam until some factory boss
cupped my waist, drank me efficiently in the morning
in Michigan and I became the hot quiet inside him.
I woke up wanting to stand in the wind
and wave at my neighbor, Peg, who photographs ball games
all day, she does this for a living, bends light onto film and looks
so hard at her work the chests of athletes blaze above her
like candescent lake birds in her sleep,
                            but I'm telling you
I'm standing in the sunshine, right now, at my window,
I'm hearing pine trees typing on my house,
I'm watching geese pound over, I can feel the way they want the smell
of the deep south, the cold of Michigan driving them, the way
I want the smell of the candy-blue light of every late night
drive thru and backseat of my life, every Jennifer
who sat with me and cried into the carbonation
of her Coke, which is exploding, right now, still, inside
my mouth, I can feel it, all of the water in Michigan can feel it,
it calls me to the green fire of the television every night,
the pop-country music of the American language, the cadence
of the advertisers, the cadence of the speeches of the automakers,
the whole of the steel and coal of Detroit hardening back into fossil,
creaking with the rusty song of the end of things, I mean all of our deaths,
the way our hipbones like hubcaps will roll off into
growling streets, which is just the growl of the beginning
of things, which is just the awkward, unforgettable tune
I want to play, right now, I'm telling you, on the ice-white piano of Michigan.

Alfred Sisley: *Snow at Louveciennes*

Alfred, the wind in your world
lopes, snow-drunk.
A lone woman walks in it,
her apron scattering salt

brought from her bright kitchen, its white
joining white the way your canvas
leaks through the tops of clouds,
clumps up where snow clumps, in branches,

on the fence. Her face is itself a clump
of color, featureless beneath her black
umbrella bowing to three bare trees,
the only bending thing here despite

the white weight. You have made everything
upright but unanchored, houses foundationless,
trees with no roots, fences sliding
in place, even her shoes floating

somehow over the snow-vague ground.
What has she come for, out of the warmth
of her house? Does she walk toward
me, carrying some message?

I have read about your throat cancer,
the shame your father felt
losing his money, your life of penury.
I have come here to your street, your fences, your trees,

to this place where nothing touches the ground,
where a woman moves against the cold
with what looks to me like joy. I, too,
have come to watch smoke drift out of houses.

Author Bio

Jeffrey Bean was raised in Bloomington, Indiana. Currently, he lives with his wife Jessica and daughter Olivia in Mount Pleasant, Michigan, where he is an associate professor of English/Creative Writing at Central Michigan University. His first full length collection, *Diminished Fifth*, was published by David Robert Books in 2009. His poems have been featured on The Writer's Almanac, and in Garrison Keillor's anthology, *Good Poems, American Places*. Recent poems appear or are forthcoming in the journals *FIELD*, *Cimarron Review*, *Crab Orchard Review*, *Subtropics*, *Smartish Pace*, and *River Styx*, among others.